Amen

The Story of Scripture from Eden to Eternity

by KRISTIN SCHMUCKER

STUDY SUGGESTIONS

Thank you for choosing this study to help you dig into God's Word. We are so passionate about women getting into Scripture, and we are praying that this study will be a tool to help you do that. Here are a few tips to help you get the most from this study:

• Before you begin, take time to look into the context of the book. Find out who wrote it and learn about the cultural climate it was written in, as well as where it fits on the biblical timeline. Then take time to read through the entire book of the Bible we are studying if you are able. This will help you to get the big picture of the book and will aid in comprehension, interpretation, and application.

• Start your study time with prayer. Ask God to help you understand what you are reading and allow it to transform you (Psalm 119:18).

• Look into the context of the book as well as the specific passage.

• Before reading what is written in the study, read the assigned passage! Repetitive reading is one of the best ways to study God's Word. Read it several times, if you are able, before going on to the study. Read in several translations if you find it helpful.

• As you read the text, mark down observations and questions. Write down things that stand out to you, things that you notice, or things that you don't understand. Look up important words in a dictionary or interlinear Bible.

• Look for things like verbs, commands, and references to God. Notice key terms and themes throughout the passage.

• After you have worked through the text, read what is written in the study. Take time to look up any cross-references mentioned as you study.

• Then work through the questions provided in the book. Read and answer them prayerfully.

• Paraphrase or summarize the passage, or even just one verse from the passage. Putting it into your own words helps you to slow down and think through every word.

• Focus your heart on the character of God that you have seen in this passage. What do you learn about God from the passage you have studied? Adore Him and praise Him for who He is.

• Think and pray through application and how this passage should change you. Get specific with yourself. Resist the urge to apply the passage to others. Do you have sin to confess? How should this passage impact your attitude toward people or circumstances? Does the passage command you to do something? Do you need to trust Him for something in your life? How does the truth of the gospel impact your everyday life?

• We recommend you have a Bible, pen, highlighters, and journal as you work through this study. We recommend that ballpoint pens instead of gel pens be used in the study book to prevent smearing. Here are several other optional resources that you may find helpful as you study:

• www.blueletterbible.org This free website is a great resource for digging deeper. You can find translation comparison, an interlinear option to look at words in the original languages, Bible dictionaries, and even commentary.

• A Dictionary. If looking up words in the Hebrew and Greek feels intimidating, look up words in English. Often times we assume we know the meaning of a word, but looking it up and seeing its definition can help us understand a passage better.

• A double-spaced copy of the text. You can use a website like www.biblegateway.com to copy the text of a passage and print out a double-spaced copy to be able to mark on easily. Circle, underline, highlight, draw arrows, and mark in any way you would like to help you dig deeper and work through a passage.

1 *God*

REVEALED IN 3 PERSONS.

FATHER, SON, & HOLY SPIRIT

66 BOOKS

that make up 1 book

3 *languages*

HEBREW | GREEK
ARAMAIC

WRITTEN OVER APPROXIMATELY

1500 *years*

1,189 *chapters*

OLD

2 TESTAMENTS

NEW

27

New Testament *Books*

approximately

40 WRITERS

{1} *DIVINE* AUTHOR

39

Old Testament *Books*

How sweet *your word* is to my taste — *sweeter than honey* in my mouth.

———

Psalm 119:103

BOOKS *of* the BIBLE

OLD TESTAMENT

Law

History

Poetry

Major & Minor Prophets

—

Intertestamental Period

—

NEW TESTAMENT

Gospels

History

Letters

Prophecy

Genesis	Isaiah	Romans
Exodus	Jeremiah	1 Corinthians
Leviticus	Lamentations	2 Corinthians
Numbers	Ezekiel	Galatians
Deuteronomy	Daniel	Ephesians
Joshua	Hosea	Philippians
Judges	Joel	Colossians
Ruth	Amos	1 Thessalonians
1 Samuel	Obadiah	2 Thessalonians
2 Samuel	Jonah	1 Timothy
1 Kings	Micah	2 Timothy
2 Kings	Nahum	Titus
1 Chronicles	Habakkuk	Philemon
2 Chronicles	Zephaniah	Hebrews
Ezra	Haggai	James
Nehemiah	Zechariah	1 Peter
Esther	Malachi	2 Peter
Job	Matthew	1 John
Psalm	Mark	2 John
Proverbs	Luke	3 John
Ecclesiastes	John	Jude
Song of Solomon	Acts	Revelation

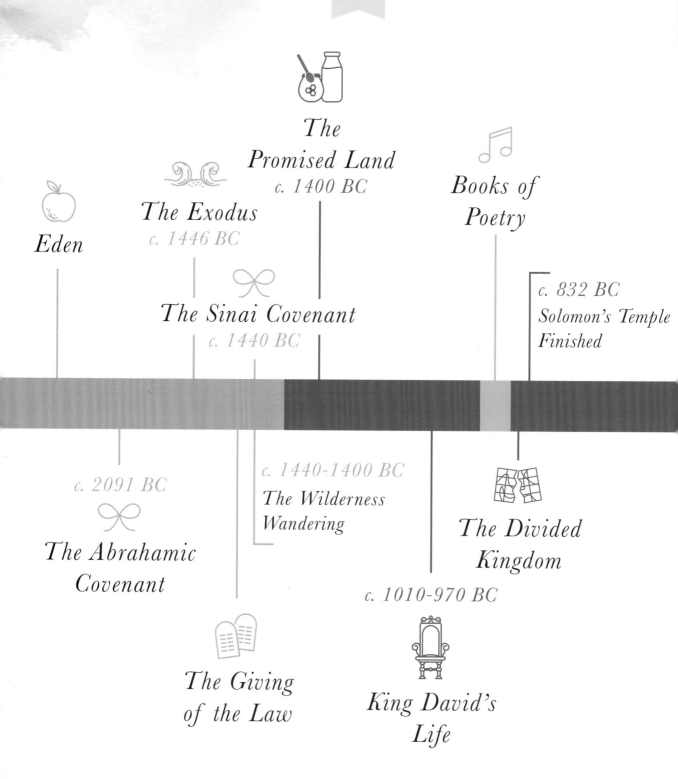

The Timeline of Scripture

The Promised Land
c. 1400 BC

Books of Poetry

The Exodus
c. 1446 BC

Eden

c. 832 BC
Solomon's Temple
Finished

The Sinai Covenant
c. 1440 BC

c. 2091 BC

c. 1440-1400 BC
The Wilderness
Wandering

The Divided
Kingdom

The Abrahamic
Covenant

c. 1010-970 BC

The Giving
of the Law

King David's
Life

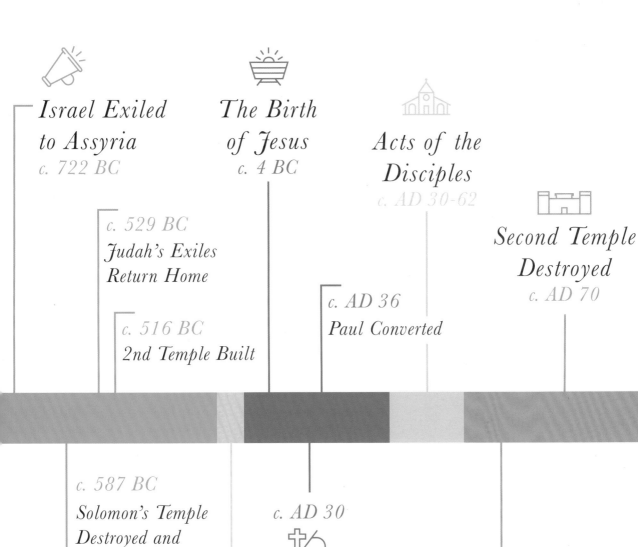

Israel Exiled to Assyria
c. 722 BC

The Birth of Jesus
c. 4 BC

Acts of the Disciples
c. AD 30-62

Second Temple Destroyed
c. AD 70

c. 529 BC
Judah's Exiles Return Home

c. 516 BC
2nd Temple Built

c. AD 36
Paul Converted

c. 587 BC
Solomon's Temple Destroyed and Judah's Exile to Babylon

c. AD 30

Jesus' Death

The Letters

{shhh}
The Intertestamental Period

Why the Bible is Important

We are embarking on a study of the Story of Scripture. We will seek to have a greater understanding of God's plan and purpose for all of history, and in the process we will be reminded that He has a plan and purpose for us as well. The Story of Scripture is going to teach us that we can trust our God. Before we begin to look closely at the Story of Scripture, we must take a moment to look at the importance of Scripture and ask ourselves why the Bible is important. As we approach God's Word it is helpful to have an understanding of the Bible itself. God's Word is inspired, inerrant, sufficient, and eternal.

Scripture is inspired by God. It is fully accurate and proven for centuries. It is not the product of men, but it is the product of God (2 Peter 1:21). It does not just contain truth; it is the truth (I Thessalonians 2:13). 2 Timothy 3:16-17 shows that all Scripture is given by inspiration; it has been "breathed out" by God. The Bible does not just contain the Word of God—it *is* the Word of God. Though God used men to write down the words of Scripture, the words are actually the words of God. There is no part of the Bible that is not inspired by God.

Scripture is inerrant. This means that it is without error. It is completely true. Everything recorded in it is accurate. God does not lie, and everything He has recorded in His Word is true (John 17:17, Titus 1:2, Hebrews 6:18). The original manuscripts of Scripture were breathed out by God Himself and without contradictions, discrepancies, or errors of any kind. God's Word can be trusted, because God can be trusted.

Scripture is sufficient. It contains everything we need for life. It is profitable (2 Timothy 3:16-17). It is all that we need to know about who God is. We don't need to look for any other revelation, because He has already given us everything that we need in His Word. The Word of God points us to the gospel, and the gospel changes everything.

Scripture is eternal. It stands the test of time and will never fade away. God has promised that He will preserve His Word, and He has been faithful to that promise (Psalm 12:6-7, Psalm 119:89-91, Matthew 5:18). The Bible is not an outdated book, but it is enduring truth.

When we begin to grasp the significance of Scripture and we recognize that it is a gift to us, our hearts will desire to open this sacred text and read it. We do not read to simply learn some nice stories or even to solve all of our problems. We come to the Bible to learn who God is and be transformed into His image through the power of His Spirit and the power of the Word of God. The Bible has accomplishing and transforming power in the life of the believer (Isaiah 55:10-11). As we come to this study, we pray that God will transform us into His image through the power of His Word.

Read 2 Timothy 3:16-17 and record why God's Word is profitable.

How does God's Word equip us for every good work?

If we fully grasped the importance of God's Word, how would our lives change?

Week 1 Day 2

Why the Story of Scripture is Important

Whether you are a new believer or someone that has grown up in the church all of your life, the Story of Scripture is something that is important to know. But unfortunately, it is often something that we struggle with. Many of us are overwhelmed by the books of the law or all of those prophets. Some of us have heard many stories and sermons through our lives, but it all seems disjointed and we don't quite understand how it all fits together.

From Genesis to Revelation, the Bible tells us one story through hundreds of stories. Scripture tells the story of redemption. It reminds us of who we are and teaches us of the God who has pursued us from the beginning of time. Despite all the times we have failed, He has remained faithful. In the first pages of Genesis, we see the promise of the Redeemer that would come and make everything right. His name is Jesus—and He changes everything. We learn about Him throughout the entire Old Testament. Then in the New Testament He bursts onto the scene, and we are overwhelmed with who He is. The Bible is the story of our redemption.

The Story of Scripture is important because when we understand it, we can understand who God is and how He works. It points us to God's plan through the ages to restore the brokenness and sin that was brought into the world at the fall, and it points us forward to a day when all that has been marred and broken by sin and death will be restored. It is the story of God pursuing the glory of His name and the hearts of His people. The Story of Scripture is important because it is our story. In it we see how our own life fits into the story of the ages that God is writing, and our hearts are encouraged to trust Him in the process.

When we begin to understand the one story seen in the Bible, it may just feel like a lightbulb goes off in our head as we see how every piece of the puzzle fits together. We will see a covenant-keeping God show covenant love to His covenant people. As we look on, our hearts will be filled with the hope of the gospel and left in awe of our God. The flame of hope is fanned as we open our Bibles. Our faith is grown as we see the story unfold, and we stand in awe of a God who does not neglect the details and is working behind the scenes to bring about His perfect plan.

There is comfort, peace, conviction, transformation, and overflowing hope to be found on the pages of Scripture, because it is in this great story that we discover the character of our God.

What parts of the Bible are you most familiar with?

What parts of the Bible are you less familiar with? What parts confuse you?

Take a moment to read and reflect on Isaiah 55:6-13 and record any observations about God's character and about His Word found in this passage.

What is the Gospel?

As we begin to study the Story of Scripture, it is helpful for us to think through a very brief overview of the gospel message so that we are able to identify it throughout the Story of Scripture.

In many ways it is the gospel message that we will be exploring further as we study through the Story of Scripture. The message of the gospel in Scripture begins in Genesis 1 as we are introduced to the all-powerful God of creation. By Genesis 3, we are introduced to the fall of humanity through Adam and Eve in the garden of Eden. Just three chapters into the grand narrative and we are already exposed to the depths of the depravity of man in doubting the Creator and then seeking to hide their sin. But God in His great mercy provided a glimpse of what was to come immediately after the devastation of the fall by giving a promise that there would come a day when the seed of the woman would rise up and crush the head of the serpent. The fall plummeted the human race into sin, and we are not immune from this. Romans 3:23 tells us clearly that we have all sinned, and Romans 6:23 makes it clear that the penalty for that sin is death.

Our God did not leave us alone in our sin with no hope. That first veiled promise in Genesis 3 would point toward the coming of Jesus, the Promised Messiah who would crush the head of that serpent and destroy the power of sin and death at the cross. Jesus entered the world as a humble Jewish baby born into the line of David. He lived the sinless life that we could not live, and He died the death that we deserved on the cross. He became sin for us so that we could be declared righteous before God (2 Corinthians 5:21). Through the death and resurrection of Jesus, we find life.

The gift of salvation is not something we can earn or achieve. There are no good works we can do or no amount of religion that will save us. Salvation is accepted by grace through faith in the finished work of Jesus (Ephesians 2:8-9). He has paid the price that we never could on our own. In His overwhelming grace He has pursued the hearts of His people. In His mercy He has not given us what we deserved. He simply asks us to accept the grace that He has given. As believers, we now live in the hope that we have found in the gospel. We rest in His finished work of redemption and look forward to the return of Christ, the restoration of all that has been tainted by sin, and the joy of dwelling in the presence of our God forever.

Has there ever been a time that you have accepted God's gift of salvation? Describe it below.

How do you think an understanding of the message of the gospel helps us to understand the story of the Bible?

How should we live in response to the gospel and the gift of grace that we have been given?

Week 1 Day 4

The Old Testament

Before we dive into the Story of Scripture, we will spend some time thinking on the structure and layout of our English Bibles. Our English Bible is made up of sixty-six books that make one book and tell one story. Today we begin with the Old Testament. The Old Testament is comprised of thirty-nine books in five categories. Understanding the categories and genres that a particular book is in will greatly help us to observe and interpret the meaning of the passages found within those books.

The first category is the law. These books are also known as the Torah or the books of Moses because they were all written by Moses. This section is found at the very beginning of our English Bibles and is filled with foundational truth. The books contained in the law are Genesis, Exodus, Leviticus, Numbers, and Deuteronomy.

The next category is that of history. These are books of theological history. They contain much information about the political and social aspects of the nation of Israel, but they also focus on the spiritual aspect of the nation and explain to us the spiritual climate of the nation and of its leaders at any given time. The majority of the chronology of the Old Testament falls within the books of the law and the books of history. The majority of the events described in the books of poetry and prophecy took place during the books of history. The books that comprise the history section are Joshua, Judges, Ruth, 1 and 2 Samuel, 1 and 2 Kings, 1 and 2 Chronicles, Ezra, Nehemiah, and Esther.

Next we have the books of poetry. These poetic books point us to the nature and character of God revealed in the world. From songs of praise to short proverbs of wisdom, the poetic books can often give us a greater understanding of what was happening in the hearts of some of the characters that we meet in the books of history. The poetic books are Job, Psalms, Proverbs, Ecclesiastes, and Song of Solomon.

The major prophets are next. The major prophets are the longer books of prophecy. All of the prophets prophesied during the times that are recorded in the books of history. They brought a message of repentance and hope to the people. The major prophets are Isaiah, Jeremiah, Lamentations, Ezekiel, and Daniel.

The last category of the Old Testament books is the minor prophets. They are called minor prophets due to their compact size. The message of the minor prophets is the same as the major prophets. It is a message of repentance and messianic hope. The minor prophets are Hosea, Joel, Amos, Obadiah, Jonah, Micah, Nahum, Habakkuk, Zephaniah, Haggai, Zechariah, and Malachi.

We will begin to explore these sections more closely, but an overview of the sections will be beneficial in helping us grasp the story.

Which section of the Old Testament are you most excited to learn more about?

Your reading today is a variety of passages from each of the sections in the Old Testament. Read each passage and then record any thoughts on their differences and similarities.

Why do you think it is important to understand the structure of the Bible? How will this help you as you study different portions of Scripture?

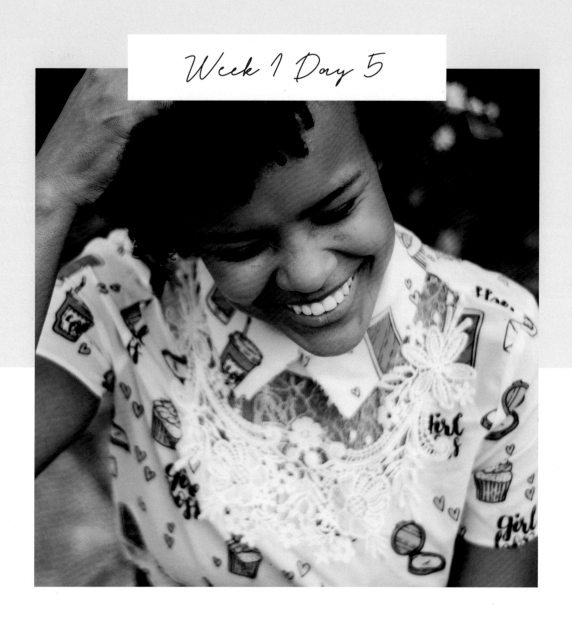

The New Testament

Today we will spend time considering the structure of our New Testament. The New Testament is comprised of twenty-seven books in four categories, and we have about 430 years between the end of the Old Testament and the beginning of the New Testament.

The first category that is found in the New Testament is the Gospels. The Gospels are Matthew, Mark, Luke, and John. These four books all look at the life and teachings of Jesus. Three of the Gospels are considered to be synoptic. These are Matthew, Mark, and Luke. They take a very similar approach and give a different perspective on many of the same events. The book of John is not considered to be one of the Synoptic Gospels, and it takes a very theological and slightly different approach than the other Gospels. The Gospels reveal Jesus as the Messiah. They show Him as the Glorious King, the Suffering Servant, the Son of Man, and the Son of God.

The next category is history, and the book in this category is the book of Acts. The book of Acts is the history of the early church and shows what happened after the resurrection of Jesus. In it we see the ascension, the sending of the Holy Spirit, the conversion of the apostles, and the mission of the church go forward.

The next category is the largest in the New Testament. The letters or epistles comprise twenty-one books of the New Testament. These are letters to churches and individuals that give instruction in theology and practical Christian living. The books contained in the letters are Romans, 1 and 2 Corinthians, Galatians, Ephesians, Philippians, Colossians, 1 and 2 Thessalonians, 1 and 2 Timothy, Titus, Philemon, Hebrews, James, 1 and 2 Peter, 1, 2, and 3 John, and Jude.

The last category in the New Testament is prophecy, and this is the book of Revelation. The book of Revelation is a book that gives details about the consummation of God's plan for history, and it is a book that gives us a beautiful picture of worship as it points our focus to Jesus who has fulfilled every promise of Scripture.

As we begin our study of Scripture we will see how each section of the story points to Jesus, and we will be reminded of the love and faithfulness of our great God.

What section of the New Testament are you most excited to learn about?

Today you are reading a variety of passages from each of the sections in the New Testament. Read each passage and then record any thoughts on their differences and similarities.

Next week we will begin to dive into the Story of Scripture. Write out your prayer as you embark on this journey to understand God more through the story of the Bible.

Week 1 Memory Verse

For just as rain and snow fall from heaven and do not return there without saturating the earth and making it germinate and sprout, and providing seed to sow and food to eat, so my word that comes from my mouth will not return to me empty, but it will accomplish what I please and will prosper in what I send it to do.

Isaiah 55:10-11

Week One
Reflection Questions

Why do you think studying the story of the Bible is important?

What did you observe this week about God and His character?

What stuck out to you most in this week's study?

Write out a summary of the message of the gospel below.

How can you respond to the Scripture studied this week with personal application?

What specific action steps can you take to apply what you have learned this week?

Creation — Genesis 1 – 2

We start at the very beginning. The very first verse on the very first page starts with God. We see God create the world from nothing, and we see the magnificent artistry of the Creator. From the start, we learn that God is a God of order as He speaks the world into existence. We are being pointed to one Creator who will be revealed throughout Scripture in three Persons. We see that God is all-powerful and above all. Even Genesis 1:26 points us to the mystery of the Trinitarian God. Though Genesis 1-2 is known as the creation account, the greatest thing about these chapters is how they point to the Creator God.

Day after day God creates different aspects of the world and declares that it is good. Everything that is created by God is good and created for a purpose. On the sixth day, God creates man, and man is declared to be very good by the Creator. Humanity is set apart from the rest of creation and made in the image of God (Genesis 1:26). The man and the woman are given a command to be fruitful and fill the earth, and they are commissioned to tend and keep the garden. The entire world that God had created is entrusted to the man and the woman that God had made in His image.

After God created the world, He rested out of satisfaction to enjoy the work that He had completed. The entire earth is a display of God's glory, and after finishing the work of creation, God rests in that glory.

Genesis 2 will show us an expansion and further description of what God did in Genesis 1. It is in this chapter that we see further explanation of the creation events and of the creation of man and woman. It is here that Adam names the animals and also recognizes that he is unique among all created beings. God then puts him to sleep and creates woman from the rib of Adam. When the chapter ends, we see man and woman set in the garden to work and keep it. They were naked and unashamed.

The Garden of Eden was a picture of shalom—a picture of the peace and wholeness that is found in the presence of God. We see God dwelling with man in communion. This theme of God seeking to dwell with man will be seen all throughout Scripture. There is no sin or brokenness in the garden. In so many ways, this is what our hearts long for. We long for Eden. We yearn for unbroken communion. We yearn to live without shame. Eden points us to what once was. But it also points us to what will be again someday. It reminds us of our own longing for that shalom peace that is found in communion with God. These chapters make us long to know the majestic Creator and long to return to Eden.

What do we learn about God in the creation narrative?

Read Psalm 19:1. How does creation point to the glory of God?

In what ways does humanity yearn for peace? How do you think the sin that is present in the world impacts this desire for peace?

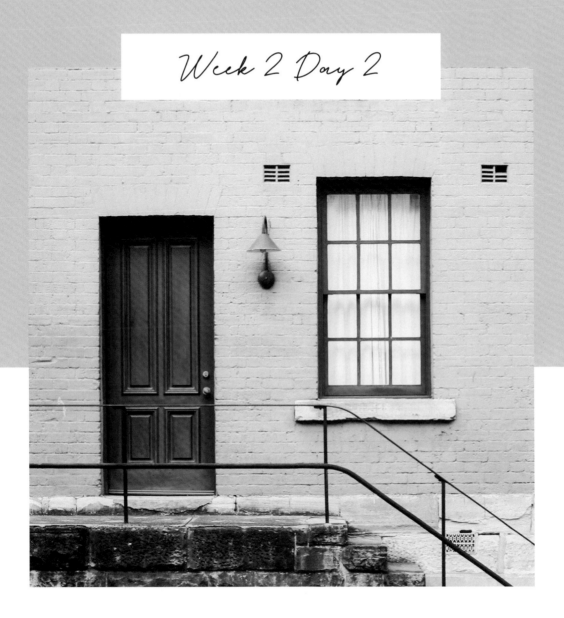

Week 2 Day 2

The Fallen World — Genesis 3 – 11

We finished yesterday with a picture of shalom peace in Eden. But it wouldn't be long before that peace was broken. As we turn the page to chapter 3 of Genesis, we watch on as tragedy strikes the world. In the midst of the garden, a single sin would change all of history. The serpent comes to deceive Eve and make her doubt God's character and what He has said. As Eve bites that fruit and hands it to Adam who is looking on, everything changes. Sin has come, and shalom has been broken. Satan must have rejoiced as Eve lifted that fruit to her lips, but what he didn't know was that God was already working. God had a plan before the ages to redeem the people that He loved (Ephesians 1:3-7, Acts 2:23). God was not surprised by the devastating sin of the first humans. This moment of depravity would set into motion the plan of redemption as the Story of Scripture unfolds.

Genesis 3 feels heavy. We are struck by the weight of the sin of the parents of humanity, and we are reminded of the weight of our own sin as well. Yet in the midst of Genesis 3 we find the promise of a Redeemer. It is a mysterious promise that redemption is coming. Genesis 3:15 is referred to by scholars as the protoevangelium because it is the first mention of the gospel. In the midst of a chapter that tells of the fall and of the consequences of sin, we see a promise. Even the devastation of the fall is drenched in gospel hope. So in a passage of Scripture titled "the curse" comes the greatest blessing mankind has ever known. Even the curse is full of blessing with our good and gracious God.

Genesis 3:15 tells us that though Satan would bruise the heel of this promised seed of the woman, this seed who is Jesus Himself would crush the head of Satan. So in one verse, God reveals the whole plan of Scripture. Satan would fight against God but only ever bruise His heel, but God would defeat Satan with a crushing blow to the head—one from which Satan would never recover.

This chapter contains a great promise of hope, but it also tells of the consequences and devastation brought about from sin entering the world. Adam and Eve would be covered by God with garments of skins which is pointing us toward a greater need for our sin to be covered by a sacrifice. Our hearts break as we watch Adam and Eve driven from the garden and separated from God. Every aspect of their lives and of the world is now marred by their sin.

Sin always brings death. It isn't always immediate, but it is a consequence of the fall. The next chapters of Genesis reveal this in vivid detail. Only one chapter after the fall we see Adam's own son kill his brother. In chapter 5, we see a list of genealogies and notice that because of sin people live and then they die. The proceeding chapters go on to give a clear picture of how sin has fractured the world. From the story of Noah to the Tower of Babel where the people try to make a great name for themselves, the devastation of sin is evident.

The impact of sin is everywhere, but the promise of the Redeemer is still there. God is still working. Though the world has been changed and peace has been broken, there is a promise that one day the Prince of Peace would come and restore all that has been broken by sin.

Contrast the environment of Genesis 1-2 with what is seen in chapter 3.

Genesis 3:15 is the first promise of the Messiah. In this one verse, God reveals the whole plan of Scripture. Paraphrase the verse below.

What does this part of the story teach you about who God is?

Covenant God — Genesis 12 – 50

We find ourselves in Genesis 12, and it shows us the call of a man named Abram whose name would later be changed to Abraham. God calls him to leave his country and his family and go to a promised land, and there have a new family and create a new nation. God's promises were great and included a great nation, a great name, blessing for Abraham, blessing for those that would bless him, and cursing for those that would dishonor him. This section of Scripture is referred to as the Abrahamic Covenant, and God would keep every single promise.

But there was one more promise made to Abraham that day. God promised a Messiah. God promised Jesus. God promised that a blessing would come through Abraham's line that would extend to all the world. This Promised One would be the One to fulfill every other promise of Scripture. Because every promise finds its "yes" and "amen" in Jesus (2 Corinthians 1:20). Jesus would be the blessing that would come to all nations. In so many ways this promise to Abraham is just an expansion of the promise that was made to Adam and Eve in Eden. Messianic hope is being imprinted on the hearts of God's chosen people.

We must remember that when these promises were made, Abraham was not the father of a great nation or the patriarch that we know of today. He was just an ordinary man chosen by God to be a part of this extraordinary story of redemption. So he obeyed and he trusted God even though he didn't understand exactly how this plan was going to work out. Abraham would have a son, and the birth of that son to a couple in their old age would be a miracle fulfillment of God's promise. The fulfillment of the promise of Isaac would serve to point Abraham and all of the world to the greater fulfillment of the promised Son of God. Abraham left the security of everything that he knew to follow God, and aren't we have so thankful that he did! Abraham's obedience was part of God's plan to bring Jesus who would rescue us from our sin once and for all.

The rest of Genesis unfolds as the descendants of Abraham begin to multiply just as God had promised and we trace His descendants through Isaac, Jacob, and his sons. The problem of sin persists through the remaining chapters of Genesis, but we also begin to glimpse the promises of this covenant unfold. These promises were not dependent on Abraham or on his descendants, but on God alone.

The story of Abraham and the rest of the book of Genesis reminds us that we can trust the Lord. Even when we don't understand or we don't think that the plan makes sense, we can trust that He is working in ways that we don't see and in ways that we don't understand. Because when God makes a promise, He always keeps it.

How does Genesis 12:1-9 promise the Messiah? Read Galatians 3:7-9 to help you understand.

Read Genesis 15 for more insight into the covenant with Abraham. We see that this covenant ceremony happens while Abraham is asleep. What does this tell us about how the covenant was completely dependent on God and not on Abraham?

God made many promises to Abraham, but Abraham did not know how it was all going to work out. How does this encourage you to trust God in your own life?

Week 2 Day 4

Deliverer — Exodus

When the book of Genesis closed, the descendants of Jacob were all in Egypt where Joseph had helped the children of Israel survive a famine. Joseph had risen to great power in the land of Egypt and the start of the book of Exodus shows how God had been faithful to that long ago promise to Abraham. His children were multiplying just as God had said that they would. But in the first chapter of Exodus, we learn that a Pharaoh came to power that did not know Joseph. He looked at the ever expanding people of Israel as a threat and a menace and decreed that all Israelite baby boys be killed. God raised up during this difficult time a deliverer that would one day save his people. He was placed in a basket and floated down the Nile in an attempt to save his life, and he was found by the daughter of Pharaoh and raised as her own. God was again working behind the scenes, and it would be in the house of Pharaoh that the rescuer of Israel would grow up. God would appear to Moses in the wilderness of Midian and speak to him through a burning bush, calling Moses to rescue the people of Israel. The task seemed impossible, but nothing is impossible with God. After signs and wonders and ten plagues, God would call His people out of Egypt.

Before they left Egypt, God would institute the Passover. This significant feast was a celebration of how God had passed over the first born of Israel when they had followed the Lord and placed the blood on their doorposts. But this memorial feast did more than just look back at God's faithfulness in the past; it also looked forward to a day when Jesus would come as the true and better Passover Lamb and save His people from their sin. It looked forward to a time when John the Baptist would cry out, "Behold, the Lamb of God!" Moses delivered the people of Israel from slavery, and that deliverance served to point the people to a far greater Deliverer who would one day deliver His people from the slavery of sin.

The book of Exodus contains the story of the people's deliverance from Egypt, but it also tells us what happened when they left. We see God providing for the people in the wilderness and the people complaining at every turn. The book of Exodus is also significant because it is here that we see the beginning of the giving of the law. From the Ten Commandments given on the top of the mountain to chapters of political and civil laws to the ratifying of a covenant, the law was a turning point in the history of Israel. God was forming the nation of Israel. What had started as a single family in the land of Egypt and grown to a people of millions was now being established as the covenant people of God.

In Exodus the people will build a tabernacle for God which would be a place of worship and sacrifice. It would be the place where God would dwell. From Eden God had desired to dwell with His people. Sin marred the story in Genesis 3, but the tabernacle brought forth a new era where the people of God would have a dedicated place of worship and where God would dwell in the midst of His people. The faithful God of Israel would not abandon His children in the wilderness.

When Abraham died, he had one son with his wife Sarah. He had no idea how God would be faithful to the promise that was made in Genesis 12. In the opening of Exodus, we see God's faithfulness on display as the descendants of Abraham were now a nation of millions. How does this encourage you to trust God to be faithful to you?

Read Exodus 12 and meditate on the truth that Jesus is our Passover Lamb. How do you think the knowledge of the Passover would have influenced the people's understanding of John the Baptist calling Jesus the Lamb of God in John 1:29?

In Exodus 24, the covenant is confirmed. The scene may seem a bit odd to us as Moses sprinkles blood on the people. Read the following verses and record your thoughts on the connections below. Hebrews 9:22, Hebrews 12:24, Hebrews 10.

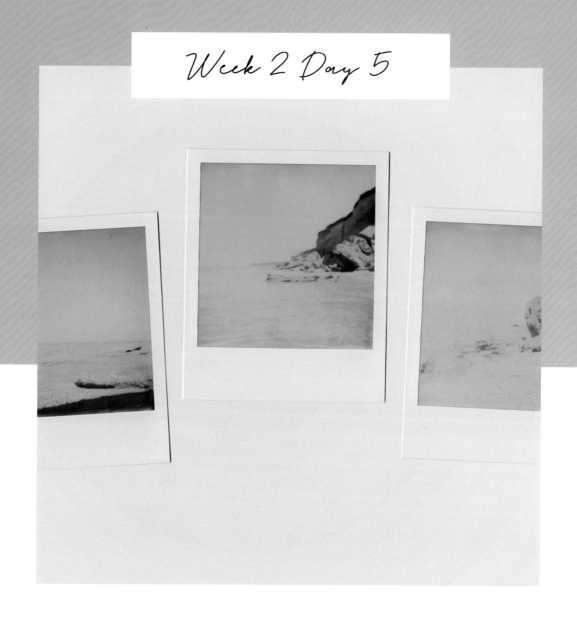

Week 2 Day 5

The Law — Leviticus – Deuteronomy

These final books of the Torah are often difficult for us to read and understand. The book of Leviticus seems bloody and confusing at first glance, but the pages of Leviticus are reminding us of all that we have already studied. Leviticus was written to the tribe of Levi and details for us the duties and office of the priest and the sacrificial system. We have already seen in our study that God is holy, that sin has a penalty, and that wherever there is sin there is death. The sacrificial system was a picture of atonement and substitution. Something had to die for the sin of the people. In the book of Leviticus, we see God accept temporary sacrifices for the sin of His people. Each sacrifice was a vivid picture of the penalty of sin. Each sacrifice reminds us that our sin has consequences. God in His mercy accepted these temporary sacrifices, but every single sacrifice was pointing to the greater sacrifice that would come in Jesus Christ who would be the once for all sacrifice (Hebrews 10:11-14). The sacrifices prescribed in the book of Leviticus had to happen over and over again, but Jesus made one sacrifice that would pay for our sin in full.

In the book of Numbers, we see the census of two different generations. The first generation is the generation that walked out of Egypt. It is the generation that walked through the Red Sea. It is the generation that had watched God be faithful at every turn. It is the generation that God was ready to usher into the promised land, and yet when we come to Numbers 13-14 we will see that it is this generation that will not trust God's power to overcome the obstacles in front of them. Though the land was flowing with milk and honey and God was ready to give it to them, all that they could see were the giants in the way. Their lack of faith would have great consequences, and this generation of the people would not be able to enter into that promised land. Instead they would wander in the wilderness for forty years. The second half of the book of Numbers will be the census of the next generation, and we are left wondering if they will make the same mistakes as the last generation. The people had been unfaithful, but God had never for a moment forgotten that unconditional promise made to Abraham in Genesis 12.

The book of Deuteronomy at first glance seems repetitive. But there is a good reason for that. The book of Deuteronomy is the retelling of the law to the new generation. This generation needed to be reminded of all that God had done for this nation. They needed to be reminded of His faithfulness. They needed to be reminded that everything that they had was because of God's gracious hand on them. Deuteronomy 6 makes this so clear for us—God wanted them to remember who He was and all that He had done. Deuteronomy 28 stands as one of the most integral chapters in the Old Testament because it helps us put the rest of the Old Testament into perspective. In Deuteronomy 28, we see blessings for obedience and consequences for rebellion. God is pleading with the people to be faithful to Him just as He had been faithful to them. But this law and its promises of blessing and abundance for obedience and hardship and confusion for disobedience did not change all that God had already promised in the Abrahamic Covenant in Genesis 12. God would keep those promises. He would faithfully accomplish all that He had promised in greater ways than anyone could imagine.

The Bible is one story, and it is coming to life for us as we begin to glimpse just a bit of what God is doing. The story of God's faithfulness in the Old Testament is also His story of faithfulness to us. May our study of this story propel us to trust Him for every moment.

Read Leviticus 1 and make note of how the sacrifices described point to Jesus who would be the greater sacrifice.

In Numbers 13-14 we look on as the people who have been surrounded by God's faithfulness choose not to trust Him. It seems so shocking, and yet we are prone to the same thing. Remembering God's faithfulness in the past helps us to trust Him for the future. Write down a few ways that God has been faithful to you.

Deuteronomy 6 speaks of God's Word being in our heart and on our lips. How can you make these things a reality in your own life?

Love the Lord your God
with all your heart, with
all your soul, and with
all your strength.

Deuteronomy 6:5

Week Two
Reflection Questions

Write a short summary of the part of the story we learned this week.

What did you observe this week about God and His character?

What did you learn about the condition of mankind and about yourself?

How did this section of the story point to the gospel?

How can you respond to the Scripture studied this week with personal application?

What specific action steps can you take to apply what you have learned this week?

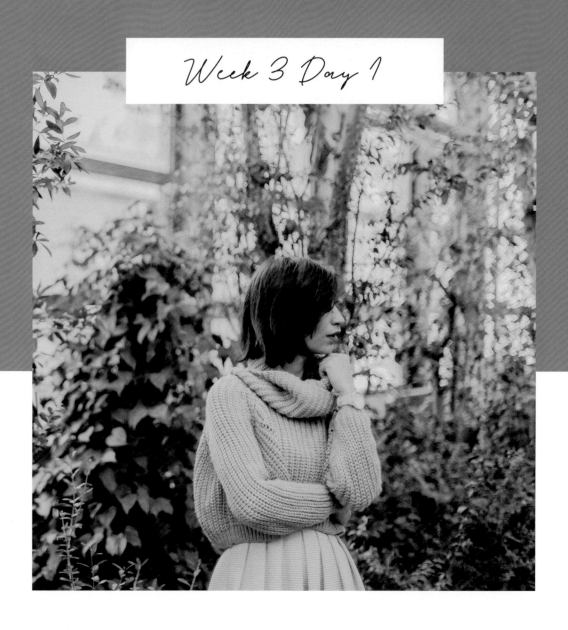

Promised Land — Joshua – Ruth

As we move out of the Pentateuch, we come to the books of history. Joshua is the first book of history, and it is all about the people going in to acquire the promised land that God had given them. It is a book of triumph as we see the conquest of Canaan and the reality that God had been faithful yet again to His people. Joshua contains triumphant accounts like the fall of the walls of Jericho and the sun standing still at Ai. It teaches us about men and women like Joshua and Rahab who believed in faith that God would keep His promises to His people. It reminds us of the persistent problem of sin with the life of Achan, but all the while it is further enforcing the triumphant faithfulness of God to bring His people into the promised land.

The book of Judges shows us the next generation of those that had entered the land. Unfortunately, Judges 2:10 tells us that this generation did not know God or all that He had done for His people. Somehow it seems that the previous generation had failed to teach the Word of God to their children like they had been commanded to do, and the results were catastrophic. The people did not follow the Lord, but instead they did what was right in their own eyes. And that meant that they rarely did what was right. The book of Judges is a cycle of sin and oppression, repentance and deliverance. Over and over and over again, the book follows this same cycle. This is a dark time in the history of Israel because it is a time when they forgot about who God was and the covenant promises that had been given to them in Deuteronomy 28. The people forfeited the blessings that would have come with obedience for the oppression and judgment that came with rebellion to God. They had made a choice, and it was the wrong one. God in His faithfulness sent judges to deliver and point them back to the Lord, but in the book of Judges it seems that time after time they ran back to the comfort of their sin.

The book of Ruth follows Judges, and the opening line of the book tells us that it took place during the time of the Judges. It records the story of a family that fled to the forbidden land of Moab during a famine. After Elimelech and his sons die, his wife Naomi is left in a foreign land with her two daughters-in-law. The book of Ruth is a story of hope from a difficult time in the history of Israel. Ruth returns with Naomi to Bethlehem where she will meet Boaz who is a picture of Jesus as our great kinsman redeemer. The beautiful story holds such a powerful meaning for us when we see it in its context beside the book of Judges. We see covenant faithfulness displayed in the life of Ruth the Moabitess. At this desperate time with no king over Israel, the book of Ruth will point us forward to the coming of the King of Kings.

The story continues, and again we are pointed to a faithful God who has not left His people. The book of Ruth specifically points us to the lineage of the Messiah. What a comfort to know that even in the midst of a season of the people's unfaithfulness, God was faithfully bringing to pass that promise from Genesis 3 and the covenant with Abraham in Genesis 12. There would be a Deliverer one day who would be greater than any judge of Israel, and He would redeem His people.

In the book of Joshua, the people finally walk into the land that God had promised to them. Describe what you think it must have been like to see the fulfillment of that promise. Have you ever had something happen after years of waiting? Is there something you are waiting on the Lord for now? Take time to ask Him to help you trust Him in this season.

In the book of Judges, a generation rises up that did not know the Lord. Read Judges 2:10 again and think about how this verse reminds us to share our faith with others and speak of His faithfulness to those around us. How can you do that?

Ruth shows us that God is working behind the scenes. How does this encourage you?

The People's King — 1 Samuel

The book of Ruth and the genealogy that it ends with are preparing us for the book of 1 Samuel. As we transition into this new era, we are introduced to a man named Samuel. We first see the story of his birth and his mother Hannah who prayed to the Lord for a child. In chapter 3, Samuel is called by the Lord. We see Samuel as a very transitional character to transition us from the period of the judges into this new era. Samuel leads the people, and he follows the Lord. In this period of time, the people are not as rebellious as they were in Judges, but they are not wholly following the Lord either. In 1 Samuel 4-7 the narrative shifts our focus to the ark of the covenant and sheds light on the condition of the hearts of the people. The people seem prone to use the ark as a good luck charm. The ark was supposed to represent God going with the people into battle, but it seems the people are more concerned about the victory the ark brings than they are with the presence of God going with them in battle and in life. So often we are prone to want the blessings of God without wanting God Himself, and that is exactly what is happening here. May we desire the Giver and not just the gifts.

It comes as no surprise then that we transition into 1 Samuel 8 where the people demand a king. They want a king, and they want him now. They do not want God to be their King, and they do not want God to be the one to choose a king. They want to set a ruler up for themselves and be just like the other nations. God had set them apart and called them to be different, but they wanted to be just like the nations that surrounded them. They demanded a king despite Samuel warning them of the words God had spoken to them in Deuteronomy 17 concerning the dangers of having a king. They persisted, and God granted them their sad request.

The people chose Saul to be their king. By the world's standards he seemed like the perfect choice. They thought that he was everything they wanted. And though things started out okay, it wasn't long before we see Saul rebelling against God's commands to him. An arrogant and prideful spirit had come along with his ascent to power, and by chapter 16 we see that Samuel is sent by God to anoint a new king. Samuel would anoint David who would be the shepherd king of Israel, but David would not immediately ascend to the throne. The young shepherd would have a long wait until he would take the throne that had been given to him by the Lord.

The rest of 1 Samuel shows David on the run from King Saul. Though David was the king that God had chosen for the people, the people were stuck with the king that they had chosen for themselves and all the chaos that he brought upon the nation. For David, the end of 1 Samuel shows a time of struggle and uncertainty, but also a time when David strengthened his heart in the Lord (1 Samuel 30:6). David didn't know what God was doing, and he didn't know that it would just be the turn of a page of Scripture before he would be anointed as king over Judah. The end of 1 Samuel for Saul shows the tragic death of Saul. Even in these chapters of kings and kingdoms, we see the covenant God and His faithfulness despite so much unfaithfulness from His people.

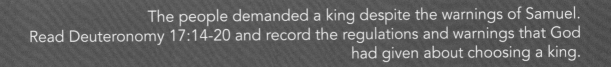

The people demanded a king despite the warnings of Samuel. Read Deuteronomy 17:14-20 and record the regulations and warnings that God had given about choosing a king.

From the outward appearance, Saul was a clear choice as king, but God sees things differently than man sees. Read 1 Samuel 16:7 and write below the difference between how God and man see.

1 Samuel shows us the big mess that the people of Israel had caused, and yet God was still working. How does this encourage you to trust God in your circumstances?

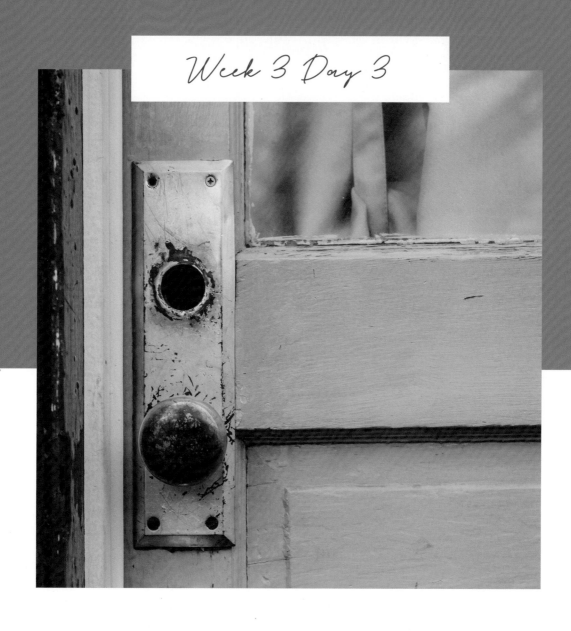

The Davidic Covenant — 2 Samuel

David was the shepherd king of Israel. He had been taken by God from the pasture to the palace. He was called a man after God's own heart. His life was not without sin, or trial, or suffering. David made many mistakes, and he had endured a life filled with both prayer and praise through suffering and joy. After seeing all that the Lord had brought him through, David had a desire to build a permanent house for the Lord. For generations, God had been worshiped in the tabernacle and then a temporary structure as a temple. But with David as the king of Israel, he desired for God's people to build a permanent and glorious temple to worship the Lord. David expresses this desire to Nathan, and though Nathan initially thinks it is a great idea, Yahweh then appears to Nathan with a covenant for David. The Davidic covenant is full of some of the most important promises from God and a more full picture of some of the promises made to Abraham.

David wanted to put God's glory on display through a temple, but God wanted to put His glory on display through David. David wanted a glorious temple, but God had other plans. David wanted to build God a house, but instead God built David a house. These verses in 2 Samuel show us the covenant between God and David. This covenant was one that was dependent on God alone. God promised that David's house and throne would be established forever. And He promised that David's seed would build a house for God's name. In the immediate sense, this was a great promise of Solomon building the temple that David had dreamed of, but David knew that this promise was even greater than that. The promise would have an ultimate fulfillment in the One who would make David's throne established forever. This was a promise of Jesus the Messiah who would come through the line of David. Only Jesus could be the true fulfillment of this forever promise (Jeremiah 23:5-6, Isaiah 9:6-7, Hebrews 1:8).

David was a sinful man who was desperately in love with God. He made many mistakes, and yet His heart for God never wavered. David would fail and sin, but this promise was not dependent on David's faithfulness but on the steadfast faithfulness of our faithful God. We may fail, but He will be faithful.

David's response to the promise of God was praise and adoration because David knew that God would be faithful to this promise (2 Samuel 7:18-29). Our God will not fail His children. He is faithful to every promise. So when the first words of the New Testament open and we see Jesus, the son of David, we are reminded that our God is faithful and true. Though we fail, yet still He is faithful. He will never fail us, and the Davidic covenant reminds us that we can trust Him. From the death of David until the coming of Jesus, David's line would face many trying days. Yet, the coming of Jesus would be a glorious reminder of how God keeps His promises and uses imperfect people to bring about His perfect plan. Though we are unfaithful, He is always faithful.

Read 2 Samuel 7 alongside the Abrahamic covenant found in Genesis 12. How are these two covenants similar?

David was imperfect, and yet he was used to bring about God's perfect plan. David was sometimes unfaithful, but God was always faithful. How have you seen God be faithful in your life?

David's response to God's promises was praise and adoration (2 Samuel 7:18-29). Take a moment to write out a prayer to God and praise Him for who He is.

Week 3 Day 4

A Broken Family — 2 Samuel – 1 Kings

Just a few chapters after the triumph of the Davidic covenant, we find the fall of the king and the consequences of sin. In the first chapters after the covenant we see the victories of David, but when we come to chapter 11, we see him at home when he should have been at war with his army. It is then that David sees Bathsheba, and his heart is filled with lust. In an abuse of his power and influence, he calls for her and commits adultery with her while her husband is on the battlefield. But sin always takes you farther than you intend to go, and soon David finds out that she is pregnant and now he chooses to cover it up. He brings Bathsheba's husband Uriah home from the battle, but his plan fails. In the end, he kills Uriah by intentionally placing him at the front of the battlefield. The prophet Nathan gives a stunning illustration of what David has done and then declares to David, "You are the man." David's sin would bring great consequence, but unlike Saul had before, David is broken by his sin and turns his heart back to the Lord. The consequences will still come, but God would remain faithful. The promises that God had made to David in chapter 7 were firm and secure despite the sin of David. Those promises were based on who God is and not on what David did.

David is succeeded by his son Solomon, and though Solomon was known for his judicial wisdom in governing the people of Israel as well as the building of a glorious temple, his personal life was full of trouble. Solomon's heart was led away from the Lord. 1 Kings 10-11 in contrast with Deuteronomy 17:14-20 are sobering and shocking as we see that God had set forth clear commands for how a king of Israel was to behave, and Solomon had rejected the law of God in favor of his own desires and pursuits. God had said that the king was not to acquire many horses, and specifically not to go to Egypt to acquire horses, but Solomon had done just that (1 Kings 10:28). God had commanded that the king should not acquire many wives, but Solomon would have 700 hundred wives and 300 concubines, and those women would pull his heart away from the Lord (1 Kings 11:3). A king was supposed to have a heart for God, but Solomon's decisions had taken him far from the Lord and there would be great consequences to pay.

The lives of David and Solomon remind us of our weakness as fallen humans. We are so prone to sin. David was a man after God's own heart, and yet we see him committing sin that leaves us stunned and speechless. Solomon built the most magnificent temple for God, and yet we see his heart turned from the Lord by his wives. And yet through it all, God is faithful. God has not forgotten His covenant. There would be consequences to pay, but God was going to do what He had promised. And really this has been the Story of Scripture so far, and it is the story of our own lives as well. We are weak, we sin, we fail, we are broken, and yet God is ever strong, holy, and faithful to bring about every word of His promise.

God used these broken men to accomplish great things and to establish the line of the Messiah. How does that encourage you to know that God can use you?

David's response to his sin was brokenness and repentance. What does this teach you about how we should respond to our own sin?

Compare 1 Kings 10-11 with the Deuteronomy 17 passage. What did Solomon do that was against these commands for how a king should live?

Learning the Story

Today take time to rewrite the story up until this point in your own words. Review any portions of the story that don't seem clear and make note of all the ways that God has been working in the story up until this point.

notes

_____

Week 3 Memory Verse

Your house and kingdom will endure before me forever, and your throne will be established forever.

―――――――

2 Sam 7:16

Week Three
Reflection Questions

Write a short summary of the part of the Story we learned this week.

What did you observe this week about God and His character?

What did you learn about the condition of mankind and about yourself?

How did this section of the Story point to the gospel?

How can you respond to the Scripture studied this week with personal application?

What specific action steps can you take to apply what you have learned this week?

Week 4 Day 1

A Song of Worship — *Job* – *Song of Solomon*

The Old Testament contains five books of poetry, and the majority of them take place here in the time of David and Solomon, with the majority being written by these two men. These poetic books point us to who God is and how He works. We see insight into God's character, and we also see insight into who we are as humans as we see people of faith wrestle with doubt, struggle, suffering, and turmoil, and yet learn to praise God in the midst of it all.

Psalms give us a beautiful picture of life with God. The Psalms are filled with lament and praise. The Psalms talk about real life. In the book of Psalms, we see descriptions of God's character that give us confidence in who He is. We also see descriptions of all that He has done. This includes references to all of Israel's history. As we examine the Psalms closely, we can see the impact of the fall on the lives of people. Sin has broken this world, and the impact of that brokenness is seen in our relationships, in our sufferings, and in every aspect of our lives. And yet it is also in the Psalms that we see so clearly that we have a Refuge and a place to run in every situation. Though the pain of life is real and ever present in our lives, the peace of God is also ever present in the life of God's people. In this life we may not always understand what God is doing or how He is working, but even in struggle we can worship Him. And we can look forward to the day when we will praise Him forever.

Proverbs is a book of wisdom. The book is filled with short proverbs of wisdom for everyday living. The book compels us to live lives that are characterized by wisdom and not folly. It instructs us to live out the law in our everyday lives.

Job, Ecclesiastes, and Song of Solomon show us the reality of life from several different angles. In Job, we see the sovereignty of God over all things and the suffering that is present in this life as a result of the fall. The book of Ecclesiastes presents a reminder that nothing in this world will satisfy other than God. The book of Song of Solomon is a book about marital love and intimacy. The book describes the beauty of marriage and sexuality in the confines of biblical marriage while reminding us that the ultimate purpose of all marriage is to point to God and His love for His people.

Though the books of wisdom and poetry may seem separate from our narrative at first glance, they are really enforcing everything that we have learned up until this point. In them we see that God is good and holy. We see that sin is real and devastating. We see that people are broken and needy. And we see that God keeps every promise and never leaves His children. These books encourage us and exhort us. They are books of poetry but also books of theology that mold and shape our understanding of who God is.

It was stated that the books of poetry are also books of theology. How is this true? How do the poetic books shape our understanding of who God is?

How do the poetic books point to the brokenness caused by sin?

What do the poetic books set forth as the remedy for that sin?

A Kingdom Divided — 1 Kings – 2 Kings

God made it clear that the kingdom would be taken from Solomon, but He also said that for the sake of David He would not do it during Solomon's life. God had been faithful, but Solomon had turned his heart from the Lord. His actions would have massive consequences not just in his own life but in the life of the nation. 1 Kings 11 tells us that though the Lord had appeared to Solomon, Solomon refused to do what God had commanded him to do. Just as the Pentateuch had said, there would be consequences for disobedience. God made it clear that the kingdom would be taken from Solomon, but also said that for the sake of David, God would not do it during Solomon's life.

What God had said quickly came to pass, and the kingdom was divided in two. The northern kingdom was referred to as Israel. It comprised ten tribes with a capital in Samaria. The southern kingdom was referred to as Judah. It was made up of two tribes and had a capital in Jerusalem. The rest of 1 and 2 Kings records for us the kings of the divided kingdom. In the northern kingdom, there were no good kings. In the southern kingdom, we see a mixture with just a few good kings. God had told the people in Deuteronomy 28 that there would be blessing for obedience. If the people obeyed, God would drive out their enemies and give them victory. But He had also warned them of the dire consequences for disobedience. If the people disobeyed the Lord and were not faithful to the covenant, God would allow their enemies to overtake them. The message of Scripture was clear—judgement was coming.

The northern kingdom fell in 722 BC to the Babylonians as recorded in 2 Kings 17. The southern kingdom persevered for a little longer due to the influence of their good kings. But in 586 BC, the southern kingdom tragically fell as recorded in 2 Kings 25.

It is hard to read. It leaves us wondering why God's people would do this. But we already know why. The divided kingdom is just one more result of living in a fallen world after Genesis 3. The brokenness of sin is displayed as we see God's people turn from Him, and the consequences of sin are exactly what God had told them that they would be. But there is good news in all of this mess. God had told them what the consequences of sin would be, and He was true to His word. But God had also made promises to His people, and covenants of His faithfulness of all that He would do, and of a Messiah that would come. Even in the midst of the heartbreak of the divided kingdom, God was working. And just as He was true to His word about the consequences of sin, He would be true to His Word about His promises as well. He would keep every one. And though we are left wondering how He will do it, we can be confident that He will. The same is true in our own lives. Sometimes we look at our own situation and don't know how God can bring good from it, but He will be true to His Word. So if there is one thing that we should take away from the Story of Scripture it is that He is faithful. He will do all that He has promised to do.

How does this part of the Story point us back to the brokenness of the fall?

What do these passages of Scripture tell you about the seriousness of sin in God's eyes?

Despite the unfaithfulness of the people, God would keep His covenant. What does this tell you about the trustworthiness of God?

Week 4 Day 3

The Prophets and Exile — Isaiah – Malachi

Repent and return. This is the message of the prophets. They called the people to repent of their sin and unfaithfulness to God and to return to Him and to the covenant. The prophets were zealous and devoted men. They were men called by God to bring the message of repentance to Israel and Judah. The prophets loved their people, and they loved the Lord. They loved the people so much that they refused to ignore the sin, idolatry, and unfaithfulness that was rampant among the people. They boldly proclaimed the message that God had entrusted to them. They lived out sermons with their lives and called the people to repentance. They gave their entire lives to preach a message that was often not received. They gave everything in God's service.

The major and minor prophets comprise the last seventeen books of the Old Testament. The designations of major and minor have nothing to do with their importance but simply refers to the length of the books that the prophets wrote. Chronologically, the majority of these prophets lived and prophesied during the period of history that we have already covered. The prophets are traditionally broken into three categories: pre-exilic, exilic, and post-exilic. This is simply a way of identifying if they gave their message before, during, or after the exile.

The exile of God's people is a tragic part of the Story of Scripture. It should not come as a shock to us though, and it should not have come as a shock to Israel and Judah either. All the way back in the Pentateuch, God had given clear instruction about the blessings for obedience and the consequences for disobedience. The consequence for turning from God was that eventually the people would be rejected from the land that God had given them. The people were well aware of the consequences of their sin, and yet they chose their sin anyway.

The prophets were pleading with the people, but it was really the Lord pleading with them. He was reminding them of who He is and all that He had done for them. Many of the prophetic books spend a great deal of time detailing God's character and pointing back to His constant faithfulness to generations of His people. It is easy for us to look at the nation of Israel and be perplexed or even disgusted by their actions. They followed their own way, despite a covenant God that pursued them. They worried, despite a God that had faithfully cared for them every step of the way. But when we are honest with ourselves, we are so often like the people of Israel. We think that we know what is best for our lives instead of trusting the Lord. We worry and complain, even though He has always been faithful. So may the message of the prophets be a message to our own hearts to turn back to the Lord day after day.

Write a summary of the message of the prophets.

Isaiah 1 beautifully shows the message of many of the prophets. There would be judgement for sin, but there was also hope for redemption. What did God ask the people to do in Isaiah 1? Look for commands that were given to the people and record them below.

Isaiah 59:2 tells us about one of the effects of sin. What had happened because of the sin of the people?

Week 4 Day 4

Hope in the Waiting — Isaiah – Malachi

Tucked inside the prophetic books are an abundance of prophecies of the coming Messiah. Even this time of the people's unfaithfulness was a time where God was pulling back the curtain of history and giving glimpses of the hope that was to come. Despite the people's unfaithfulness to the law and the covenant made with Moses, God would be faithful to His promises. The Messiah that had been promised in Genesis 3 and then to David would come. And though the people did not yet know when or how it would happen, the prophetic books are filled with glimpses of hope and details about just how this Messiah would come.

There were promises about the virgin birth (Isaiah 7:14). There were promises about how He would come through the line of David (Jeremiah 23:5-6). There were promises about what He would be like (Isaiah 9:6-7). There were promises about where He would be born (Micah 5:2-5). There were promises about how He would lead His people like a shepherd (Isaiah 40:11). There were promises of how He would suffer for His people (Isaiah 53). These promises of His first coming were also mixed with triumphant passages that described His second coming that we still wait for as believers today. There were so many prophecies and so many promises, and all will be fulfilled in Jesus.

The prophets are filled with much judgment, but they are also overflowing with gospel hope. The message of repentance is clear, but there is also a reminder of God's faithfulness and desire for the restoration of the people that He loves.

Another prominent theme that runs through the prophets is the promise of a new covenant. The glorious promise of hope can be seen in Jeremiah 31:31-34. God was promising to His people a new covenant that would be different and so much better than the old covenant. The old covenant focused on regulating the actions of the people and temporary sacrifices. It was a mirror that pointed out how they could not live up to God's standard of holiness. And though that mirror of the law showed the people their sin, it could not make them clean (Romans 3:20). And that is why they needed the Messiah to come. The new covenant would not be written on tablets of stone, but on the hearts of God's people. The new covenant would point us to a single sacrifice that would atone for sin. While the old covenant sought to change the people's actions, the new covenant would transform their hearts from the inside out.

The Old Testament ends with a glimmer of hope as a remnant of the people return to the land and rebuild the temple and the walls of Jerusalem. The post-exilic prophets call for hearts that are turned to the Lord (Ezra, Nehemiah, Haggai, Zechariah, Malachi). The Old Testament ends with a question lingering in the hearts and on the lips of God's people—"will God keep His promises?"

Hope was coming for the people of Israel and Judah—and for all the world. The message of hope found in the prophets is a reminder that though we fail, God never would. The promises of God have never been dependent on us; they are dependent on God. Jesus would be the fulfillment of every promise that was made, and He is the long-awaited Messiah that every page of the Old Testament longs for.

How does the Old Testament point to Jesus?

Read Romans 3:20. What was the purpose of the law?
How does the law point us to Jesus?

The Old Testament ends with a glimmer of hope and a season of waiting for God to fulfill what He had promised. Have you ever felt like you were in a season of waiting? How does Scripture encourage you to trust and wait on the Lord?

The Prophetic Books — Timeline & Help Sheet

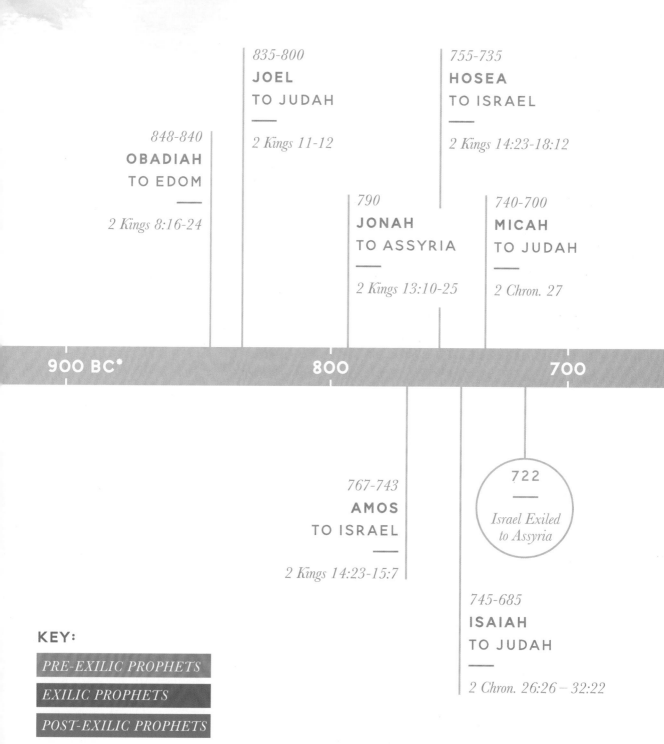

848-840
OBADIAH
TO EDOM

2 Kings 8:16-24

835-800
JOEL
TO JUDAH

2 Kings 11-12

790
JONAH
TO ASSYRIA

2 Kings 13:10-25

755-735
HOSEA
TO ISRAEL

2 Kings 14:23-18:12

740-700
MICAH
TO JUDAH

2 Chron. 27

900 BC*

800

700

767-743
AMOS
TO ISRAEL

2 Kings 14:23-15:7

722

Israel Exiled
to Assyria

745-685
ISAIAH
TO JUDAH

2 Chron. 26:26 – 32:22

KEY:

PRE-EXILIC PROPHETS

EXILIC PROPHETS

POST-EXILIC PROPHETS

*All dates are circa B.C.

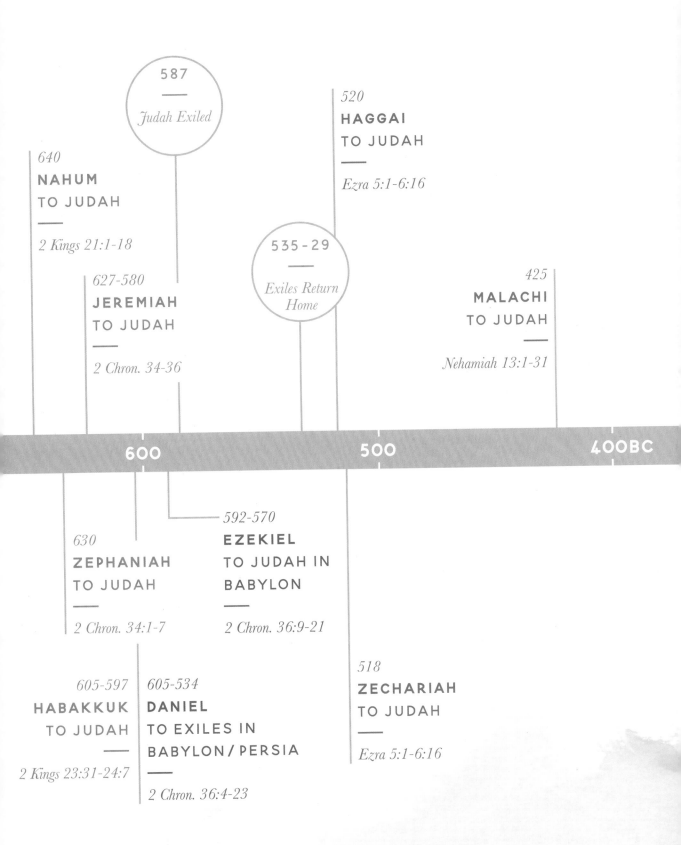

587
—
Judah Exiled

640
NAHUM
TO JUDAH
—
2 Kings 21:1-18

520
HAGGAI
TO JUDAH
—
Ezra 5:1-6:16

535-29
—
Exiles Return Home

627-580
JEREMIAH
TO JUDAH
—
2 Chron. 34-36

425
MALACHI
TO JUDAH
—
Nehamiah 13:1-31

600 **500** **400BC**

592-570
EZEKIEL
TO JUDAH IN BABYLON
—
2 Chron. 36:9-21

630
ZEPHANIAH
TO JUDAH
—
2 Chron. 34:1-7

518
ZECHARIAH
TO JUDAH
—
Ezra 5:1-6:16

605-597
HABAKKUK
TO JUDAH
—
2 Kings 23:31-24:7

605-534
DANIEL
TO EXILES IN BABYLON / PERSIA
—
2 Chron. 36:4-23

The Not So Silent Years

The period between the testaments has often been called the silent years or the intertestamental period. Yet during these 430 years, God was working and moving behind the scenes to create a situation that was ripe for the spread of the gospel in the first century. As the Old Testament ended, a remnant was able to return to the land (Ezra-Nehemiah), yet many of the people still remained scattered. The Jerusalem walls and temple were rebuilt, but things were not like they once were. Because many people did not have the ability to return to Jerusalem, synagogues began popping up throughout the region as a place where the people could hear and learn God's Word under the leadership of rabbis, or teachers of God's Word. It was during this period that religious groups such as the Pharisees and Sadducees began. It was also during this time that many Gentiles would convert or identify with the Jewish faith. Even the devastation of the exile and diaspora would serve to spread the message and people of God throughout the world, creating an environment where the gospel was ready to spread.

Assyria and Babylon had conquered the northern and southern kingdoms, but at the end of the Old Testament the empire of Persia was beginning their rule. In 334 BC, came the rise of one of the most significant world rulers when Alexander the Great rose to power. During the majority of the intertestamental period, the Greek empire was a powerhouse that took the world by storm. The period would come to be known as a period of Hellenization because the impact of Greek culture would be seen in every area of life. Most significantly would be the spread of the Greek language as a common language.

In 63 BC, Rome would conquer Jerusalem. With the coming of the Roman Empire would come the building of Roman roads that would make travel more accessible than it had ever been before.

At every step along the way in the Story of Scripture, we have seen God's faithfulness in working behind the scenes and in ways that we do not understand, and this period between the testaments is no different. God was sovereignly establishing kingdoms and moving nations to accomplish His great purpose. When the New Testament opens there is a common language (Greek), and a massive infrastructure of Roman roads that would make the spread of the gospel a possibility. The epistles of the New Testament and the message of Jesus would be carried on those roads and spoken in Greek to people all over Asia Minor that would be converted and captured by the grace of Jesus. Though 430 years is a long time to wait, God was moving and working every moment of those 430 long years that felt silent. This period reminds us to trust His plan and trust His promises. God would accomplish what He had promised, and we can trust Him to do that for us as well.

How did the events that took place during the intertestamental period prepare the way for the gospel to spread? Specifically, how would a common language and system of roads aid in spreading the gospel message?

Think for a moment about how God used the pain of the exile to bring about good. How does that encourage you in your own life?

Read Psalm 18:30 and meditate on what it means that God's way is perfect. What obstacles are there in our lives that keep us from trusting His plan?

"Instead, this is the covenant I will make with the house of Israel after those days" —the Lord's declaration. "I will put my teaching within them and write it on their hearts. I will be their God, and they will be my people.

———————

Jeremiah 31:33

Week Four
Reflection Questions

Write a short summary of the part of the Story we learned this week.

What did you observe this week about God and His character?

What did you learn about the condition of mankind and about yourself?

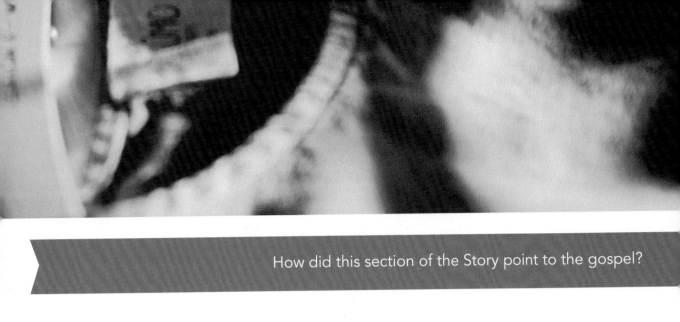

How did this section of the Story point to the gospel?

How can you respond to the Scripture studied this week with personal application?

What specific action steps can you take to apply what you have learned this week?

Week 5 Day 1

Hope Has Come — The Gospels

The first page of the New Testament opens with the declaration of what the whole world had been yearning for. The first page of Matthew begins with a genealogy. And though we are often tempted to skip these lists of names, it is in this list that we are reminded of who Jesus is. He is the promised Messiah. He is the son of Abraham and the son of David. And He is the fulfillment of the covenants made with these men. It is also in Matthew 1 that we see the reason that Jesus had come—He would save His people from their sins.

The world was longing for a savior at this pivotal time in history. Certainly the Jewish people knew the promises of the coming Messiah, but even the rest of the world found themselves longing for something as the Roman Empire sought to bring order to what had been a time of chaos. To many people in the world, Caesar Augustus seemed like a political and economic savior, and many of the Jews expected the Messiah to be this same kind of savior. One that would bring political order to Israel, but Jesus would do so much more than that.

As we read a few short and famous verses from Luke in the Christmas story, we must be left in awe of the truth that our God is always working behind the scenes bringing about His sovereign plan. His sovereign hand is seen in everything—even the decision of a Roman ruler to decree that a census was needed. It was that decree, providentially led by our God, that would lead Mary and Joseph to Bethlehem, which was the exact city that God had promised that this Savior would be born. If God can orchestrate this event and move world rulers to follow His plan, we can be confident that He is working His sovereign plan in our lives as well. Our sovereign God is at work in ways our eyes cannot see.

Many of the people were confused. Jesus did not do what they expected the Messiah to do. They were looking for a conquering king and not a suffering servant. They were looking for someone to conquer the powers of Rome, but Jesus came to conquer their hearts.

The events of the birth of Jesus the Messiah are simple and humble. While the town of Bethlehem was busy and overflowing with all those that had made the pilgrimage back to Bethlehem, a Savior was born to a young woman and placed in a manger. Mary gave birth, in less than ideal circumstances, to the One that would change everything. She swaddled the Savior of the world in strips of clothes and laid Him down in a manger made to feed animals. So often this is how our God works. He uses ordinary people and humble situations to bring about His sovereign plan. It would not be a political leader that would bring peace on earth; it would be a newborn baby who was born in a stable in a little town called Bethlehem that would come to bring peace to the hearts of His people. In the silence of that Silent Night, a Savior was born who would change everything. No one knew that God was working that night, but He was performing His greatest work for His people. If you find yourself in a silent night in your soul and life, you can know that He is working. The same baby born into that manger bed is also the conquering King and the Savior who has come to rescue.

How does the coming of Jesus remind us that God keeps His promises?

How was God working behind the scenes to bring about the birth of Jesus?

Are there areas in your own life where it may feel like God is not working? How does the coming of Jesus remind you to trust His sovereign hand?

Amen — The Gospels

Each of the Gospels gives us a picture of a different aspect of who Jesus was, and each aspect was a fulfillment of the promises of the Old Testament that Jesus fulfilled. In Matthew, Jesus is seen as the Son of David and the King of the Jews. In Mark, He is seen as the Servant as we watch Him suffer and serve for His people. In Luke, He is presented as the Son of Man as we are given glimpses of His humanity. And in John, He is revealed as the Son of God, and we are taken back to the beginning to be reminded of His deity.

As the Gospels continue, we see Jesus live the perfect life that we could never live on our own. We see Him heal the sick, cause the blind to see, and raise the dead to life. And those pictures all point us to the truth that He can spiritually heal the broken, that He can open the eyes of those blinded by sin, and that He can raise us from death to life. During His earthly ministry, Jesus was being revealed as the promised Messiah, but He was also being revealed as God Himself.

It would be Jesus' claims to be God that would push the religious leaders over the edge and cause them to seek to destroy Him. As the Gospels close, Jesus is crucified by the people He had come to save. At the moment of His death, the veil of the temple was torn in two from top to bottom. The veil had been a symbol for generations of the separation between God and man. It separated the people from the Holy of Holies. But when Jesus was sacrificed at the cross, the veil was torn as a beautiful picture that there was now access directly to God because of the sacrifice of Jesus. At the cross Jesus became the once for all atoning sacrifice for our sin. He paid the price that thousands of years of animal sacrifices could only temporarily cover.

But the death of Jesus was not the end of the story—three days later He arose victoriously over death. In Genesis 3 came the fall of humanity and the permeation of sin through every aspect of the world. But in Genesis 3:15, a promise was given of One that would come and crush the head of the serpent. The serpent would bruise the heel of the Messiah. The cross was that bruise to the heel. It was painful and excruciating, but it could not defeat Jesus. The cross was also the blow that would crush the head of the serpent. Satan will never recover from what took place at the cross. At the cross Jesus crushed Satan. The enemy has been defeated.

Every promise of the Old Testament finds fulfillment in Jesus. He is the "Amen" to all of the promises of God (2 Corinthians 1:20). Jesus is the Amen from God. He is the answer to all the brokenness and longing. He is the answer to every promise from God. He is the One that would change everything. He is the One with the power to change us.

How does the way that Jesus was presented in each Gospel give us a full picture of who He is?

How is Genesis 3:15 fulfilled?

What does it mean that Jesus is the "Amen" or the fulfillment of all of God's promises? How does that give us confidence?

Matthew

KING OF THE JEWS

Mark

SUFFERING SERVANT

Luke

SON OF MAN

John

SON OF GOD

Week 5 Day 3

The Church On The Move — Acts

The book of Acts is a New Testament book of history. It is the history of the church as it takes place after the resurrection. The book of Acts is considered to be the sequel to the book of Luke. It is the continuing story of the Gospels. The book of Acts chronicles for us many key events in the life of the church such as the ascension of Jesus and the coming of the Holy Spirit at Pentecost. It is a key book that transitions us from the Gospels and gives us a greater understanding of the setting in which the epistles or letters were written.

In Acts 1:8, Jesus promised to send the Holy Spirit just as He had spoken of in the Gospels, and He also reminded His followers of the mission that was entrusted to them at the end of the Gospels to be His witnesses to the entire world. This mission would be the mission of every believer to spread the message of the gospel to the entire world. They would begin right where they were in Jerusalem and spread to Judea, Samaria, and ultimately to the ends of the earth.

In Acts 2, the Holy Spirit would come upon believers, and Peter would boldly proclaim the message of the gospel. In His preaching he would tie together the Old and New Testaments. He would remind the people of the promises of God expressed through the prophets and remind them of the promises given to David. He would clearly explain that Jesus was the plan from before the ages began (Acts 2:23). Jesus was never plan B. In Acts 2:42, we see the believers gathering together and dedicating their lives to the teaching of the apostles and to fellowship with each other. Scripture would be the backbone of the church as believers were added daily to the body of Christ.

The book continues by showing the events that were happening in the early church. We see Stephen become the first martyr in the name of Jesus after he has recounted the story of the Old Testament (Acts 7). We are introduced to Saul who would later become the apostle Paul. When he is introduced he is a persecutor of the church, but by chapter 9 we see his glorious conversion on the road to Damascus. As the book of Acts and the church continues to move, we are reminded of how God uses even the worst things. Paul goes into the synagogues that were all over Asia Minor as a result of the exile and diaspora to bring the message of the gospel to those regions. And Paul would reach those regions via the Roman roads that had been built during the intertestamental period. All the ways that God had been working through the exile, the diaspora, and the intertestamental period were now equipping the rapid spread of the gospel.

The book of Acts is a testament to God's faithfulness to accomplish His purposes. We are encouraged by the book of Acts because these purposes are accomplished through ordinary people that surrendered to the Lord and were led by the Spirit to build God's kingdom here on earth.

Read Acts 1:8. What would happen after the coming of the Holy Spirit?

Acts 2:23-24 reminds us that Jesus was the definite and sure plan for all of time. How have we seen glimpses of that throughout the Story of Scripture?

Make a list of the things that the believers were dedicated to from Acts 2:42. How should these things be part of our lives as believers?

Week 5 Day 4

Faith and Practice — The Letters

The Epistles, or the letters, comprise the next portion of the New Testament. There are twenty-one letters that make up the majority of the New Testament books. The letters in many ways are a further expansion of the message of the Gospels and the book of Acts. They describe the foundational beliefs of orthodox Christianity. These letters written to churches and believers in the first century contain beautiful descriptions of theology as well as practical application for how believers are called to live in light of that theology. The letters are a treatise of faith and practice. They tell us who we are in Christ and how we are to live in light of that truth. The letters are a manifesto or mission statement of the church. They are a declaration that this is what we believe and this is how we are going to live.

Throughout the letters we see rich theology. Many passages gloriously explain doctrine. As is the purpose of all Scripture, the Epistles show us who God is, and they help us better understand the plan from the beginning of time of how God would rescue and redeem His people. The supremacy and sovereignty of God are central to the message of the Epistles (Ephesians 1:3-14). The deity and messianic nature of Jesus are gloriously revealed (Colossians 1:15-23, Colossians 2:9-10, 2 Corinthians 5:21). The inspiration and sufficiency of Scripture is heralded (2 Timothy 3:16, Romans 10:17, Hebrews 4:12, 2 Peter 1:21). The letters consistently point us to the depravity of man and remind us of the consequences of the fall (Romans 3:10-29, Romans 3:23, Ephesians 2:1-3). The epistles present the beauty of the gospel. They remind us of our need for atonement and point us to the One who has made the perfect atoning sacrifice for our sin (1 Peter 2:24, Hebrews 9:12, Romans 5:8-9, 1 John 4:10, Romans 3:24-26). On the pages of the letters, we are reminded that salvation is found in Jesus alone. It is a gift of His grace received in faith, and we are reminded that there is nothing that we could ever do to earn the grace that He has freely bestowed on us (2 Corinthians 5:21, Ephesians 2:8-9). The Epistles point the people of God toward the return of Christ and fill God's people with hope for the day when God's plan will be consummated (Romans 8:19-23, Philippians 3:20-21). Our theology gives us hope and assurance in the nature and character of our God.

Our theology should impact every area of our lives. The letters explain this for us. They give us a glorious view of theology (what we believe about God), and then call us to let our theology dictate every area of our lives. The message that theology should impact our lives is not just one for the first century believer. The message of the importance of theology is not just for pastors and seminary students. Every believer is called to be a theologian. And every believer is called to be transformed by their knowledge of God and His Word.

Read Ephesians 1. This chapter is rich in theological truth. Record observations about who God is and what He does below.

Read Colossians 3:1-17. Record the ways we are commanded to live in this passage below.

In what ways is every believer called to be a theologian?

Worthy is the Lamb

Every verse of Scripture points to Jesus. The Story of Scripture is the story of Jesus, the promised One who has rescued and redeemed His people. The book of Revelation is the glorious finale of this story of redemption. Our God has been writing this story since the beginning, and we have looked on as it has unfolded before us. The book of Revelation was written by the beloved apostle John during his exile on the isle of Patmos. Originally written to seven literal churches in the first century, the book magnifies Jesus at every turn. In the greeting alone we are overcome with awe at the beauty and holiness and majesty of our Prophet, Priest, and King. One glimpse of the glorified Savior causes John to fall at His feet in worship—and it should do the same for us.

The book of Revelation is centered on the truth that our sovereign God is on the throne. No event on earth has the power to move our God from His throne. He is sovereign over all, and this book pushes our hearts to worship as we see His sovereignty and glory. It is also a beautiful reminder of His faithfulness to every promise.

The book of Revelation is the grand climax of the story. It details for us the final restoration and consummation of God's eternal plan to redeem and rescue His people through Jesus. Revelation is the triumphant answer to the fall that took place in Genesis 3. In Christ alone all that was once broken by sin is redeemed and restored in Jesus. The God who sought to dwell with His people in Eden, and then in tabernacles and temples, the God who came to earth to dwell among His people as a man (John 1:14), and then in the church, now dwells in full communion with His people. The people of God will dwell with Him forever with no more tears, death, mourning, pain, sin, or crying.

So the book of Revelation and the Story of Scripture close with a call to come to Jesus. A call to come to the One who is the beginning and the end. The Genesis and the Revelation. The Story of Scripture is the story of Jesus. It is a call to come to Him and to take the water of life that He so freely has extended. So Jesus calls to all to come and taste of His grace, and then we as His children cry back to Him, "Come, Lord Jesus!" We wait, and we trust, and we rest in His grace because we know the best is yet to come. The God who has been faithful in every chapter of the story will be faithful to the end.

Every word in every verse, in every chapter, in every book, in every testament, all of Scripture has pointed to Jesus. And for eternity we will lift our voices in worship to Him and say, "Worthy is the Lamb."

Amen and Amen.

Look at Revelation 21:3. Why is it significant that the dwelling place of God will be with man?

In the glorious picture of the new heaven and new earth we see no more tears, death, mourning, pain, sin, or crying. How does this bring hope to the difficult situations that you face in your life?

What are your thoughts as you finish learning the Story of Scripture? What have you learned about God in the process?

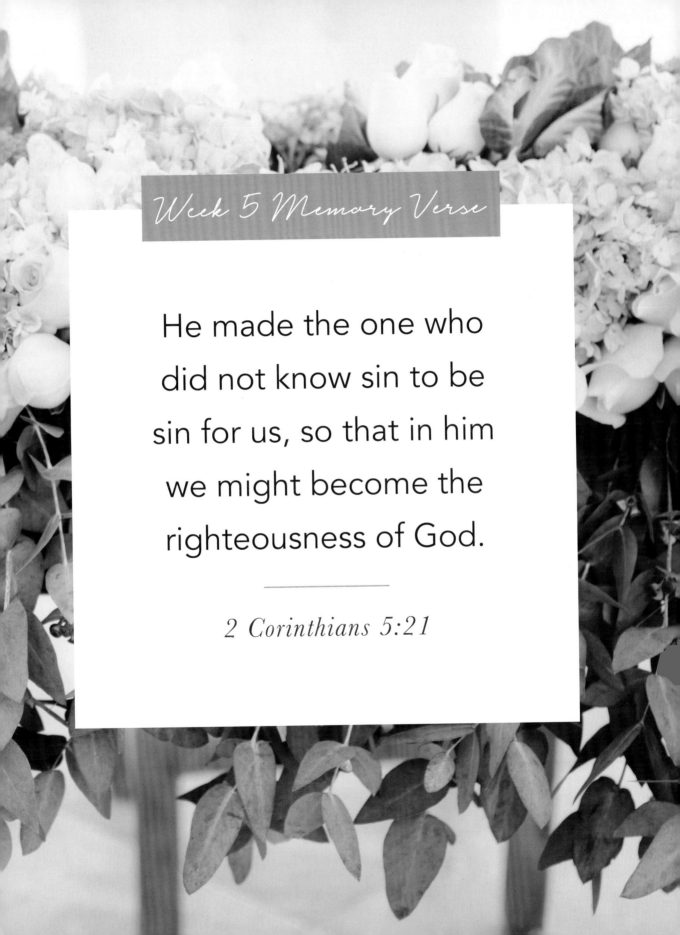

Week 5 Memory Verse

He made the one who did not know sin to be sin for us, so that in him we might become the righteousness of God.

2 Corinthians 5:21

Week Five
Reflection Questions

Write a short summary of the part of the Story we learned this week.

What did you observe this week about God and His character?

What did you learn about the condition of mankind and about yourself?

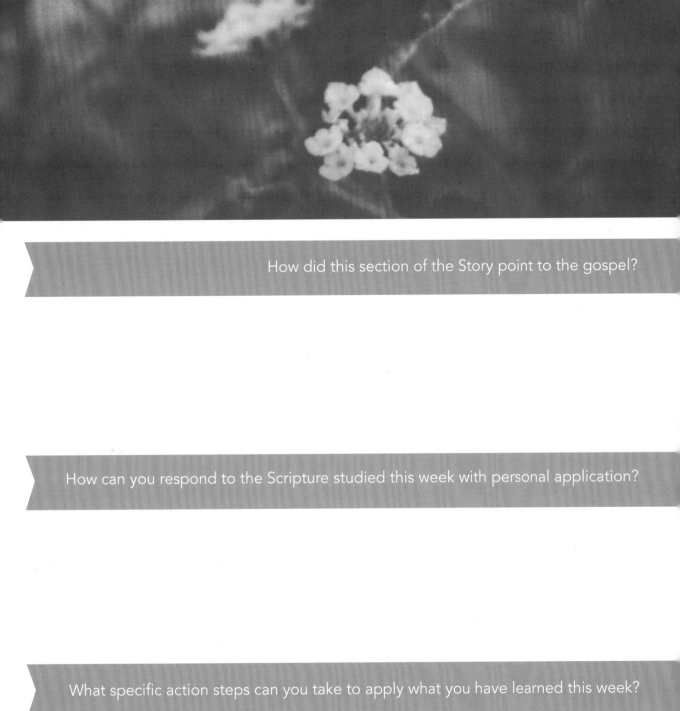

How did this section of the Story point to the gospel?

How can you respond to the Scripture studied this week with personal application?

What specific action steps can you take to apply what you have learned this week?

Rehearsing the Story of Scripture

We have come to the end of our study, and we have seen God's steadfast love and faithfulness at every turn. We have been reminded that the Bible's story is one story that finds its amen in Jesus (2 Corinthians 1:20). Jesus is salvation. Jesus is what every passage of the Old Testament and every prophecy pointed toward. Jesus is what every heart and all of the earth longed for. And He is what our own hearts yearn for as well.

There is great value in remembering the metanarrative, or big picture, of Scripture. So when we talk about the metanarrative of Scripture, we are talking about the big picture of the Bible. What is the central message and how can we explain the story of the whole Bible? One way of doing it is with four key words: creation, fall, redemption, and restoration. Identifying these themes in Scripture can give deeper insight into the text.

> *Creation* points to God and reminds us that everything started with God and that our purpose is to bring glory to God.

> The *fall* reminds us of our sin, brokenness, and separation from God. It also reminds us of how sin has caused us to live in a fallen world in which we experience sorrow, pain, and death.

> *Redemption* is the climax of the story. This is the heartbeat of the gospel, that Jesus came and died for our sins and paid the price for our redemption so that we could be reconciled to God. Redemption is the climax, but it is not the end of the story.

> *Restoration* (or consummation) is the eternal aspect of the story. This is the truth that someday, God will restore this world and dwell with His people. There will be no more sin, sorrow, or death, and we will dwell with our God and worship Him forever just as the purpose was from the beginning.

As we continue to study God's Word, we can remember the Story of Scripture. It will help us understand the biblical text better and help us to see a greater picture of who our God is and how He works.

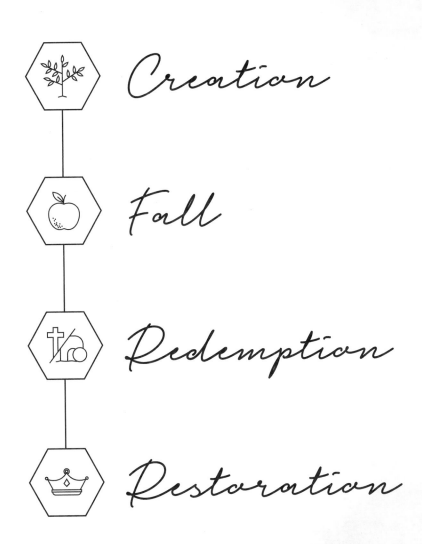

Creation

Fall

Redemption

Restoration

As we finish our study, take time to write out a summary of the Story of Scripture.

The Story of Scripture

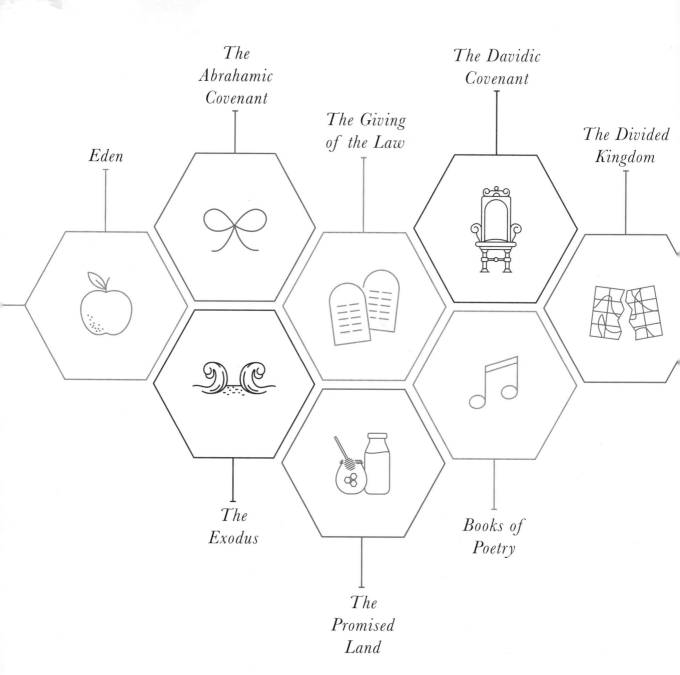

Eden

The
Abrahamic
Covenant

The Giving
of the Law

The Davidic
Covenant

The Divided
Kingdom

The
Exodus

The
Promised
Land

Books of
Poetry

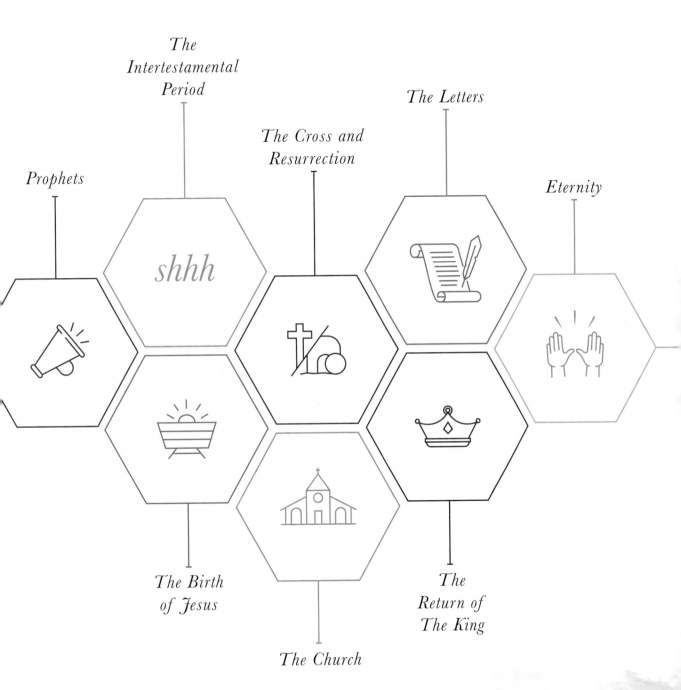

Prophets

The
Intertestamental
Period

shhh

The Cross and
Resurrection

The Letters

Eternity

The Birth
of Jesus

The Church

The
Return of
The King

FOR STUDYING GOD'S
WORD WITH US!

CONNECT WITH US:

@THEDAILYGRACECO

@KRISTINSCHMUCKER

CONTACT US:

INFO@THEDAILYGRACECO.COM

SHARE:

#THEDAILYGRACECO

#LAMPANDLIGHT

WEBSITE:

WWW.THEDAILYGRACECO.COM

———